blinis &
Crepes

Recipes by Camille Le Foll
Photography by Akiko Ida

HACHETTE
Illustrated

contents

Sweet

tips and tricks

Greasing your skillet or crêpe pan

This is one of the most important factors involved in making successful crêpes and pancakes. There are several ways to do this properly:

• Stab a medium-sized chunk of potato with a fork, dip it in oil, melted butter, or a mixture of both, and use it to spread the grease over the base and sides of the pan.

• A more traditional method lends a rustic flavor to the dish—a knob of lard or bacon fat spread by the tip of a knife.

• Simply wipe the pan with paper towels impregnated with oil in between cooking each pancake. Take care not to burn your fingers.

• Finally, for the health conscious, there are several nonstick cooking sprays available.

Making really thin crêpes

The trick is to make sure the batter is the right consistency—it should be a runny consistency, not thick. Pour a ladleful into the crêpe pan, coat the entire surface evenly, and pour off the excess batter back into the bowl to be reused.

Flavoring the batter

There are several different flavors to choose from. Here are just a few suggestions:

• Vanilla comes in different forms—as an essence, a powder, as vanilla sugar or, more luxuriously, as a bean containing the tiny seeds.

• Classic orange-flower water gives a delicate flavor. You can strengthen the taste with finely grated lemon, orange, or mandarin zest.

• Alcohol and liqueurs can be used to *flambé* or 'flame' the pancakes.

Choosing the right tools

• A cast-iron *galetière* or crêpe pan adds authenticity and local color to the procedure, but it needs regular greasing, muscle power, and dexterity.

• Nonstick skillets are recommended for beginners.

• A wooden rake helps to spread the batter evenly.

• A wooden spatula is indispensable for folding and flipping pancakes, blinis, and galettes.

• A flan mold or metal ring (available from kitchen shops) is useful for shaping crumpet batter. It should be made from reasonably heavy metal in order to remain in place in the skillet.

Wine or cider?

Wheat galettes should be accompanied by a glass of apple juice or hard cider, depending on individual taste. Buckwheat galettes go well with a glass of milk or drinking yogurt. Blinis are generally enjoyed with a glass of chilled vodka, and pancakes go down well with most drinks, in particular warm ones.

the basics

Buckwheat galettes (pancakes)

Makes around 20 galettes
1 lb buckwheat flour, sifted
1 teaspoon salt
2 eggs
water

Put the flour and salt in a bowl and make a well in the center. Beat the eggs in another bowl with two glasses of water. Gradually add the mixture of eggs and water to the flour, stirring well as you do so. Gradually add enough water to give the batter a fluid consistency.

Leave the batter to stand for at least one hour. It will thicken and develop the required texture. Dilute with a little water if necessary.

Heat an oiled cast-iron skillet and pour in a small amount of batter. Spread it immediately with a wooden rake or tilt the pan in all directions to spread a thin film of batter. Cook over a moderate heat until the pancake slides when the pan is shaken. Flip over the pancake with a spatula and cook the other side for about a minute.

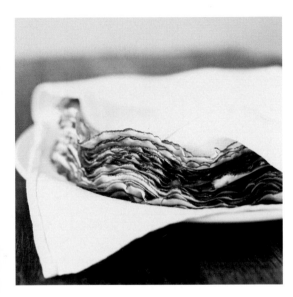

Plain flour crêpes

Makes around 20 crêpes
1³/₄ cups all-purpose flour, sifted
¹/₂ teaspoon salt
2 tablespoons sugar
3 eggs
2 cups milk
2 oz unsalted butter

Mix the flour, salt, and sugar in a bowl. Make a well in the center.

Break the eggs in a second bowl and beat, incorporating a glass of the milk. Pour the mixture into the flour well and whisk vigorously until the batter is smooth and lump-free. Melt the butter in a small pan. Add the remaining milk and melted butter, a little at a time, to the batter mixture.

Allow to stand for at least an hour.

Follow the same cooking method as for the galettes described on the opposite page.

Blinis

Makes around 12 blinis
1/2 **envelope active dry yeast**
2 1/2 **cups milk**
1 3/4 **cups all-purpose flour, sifted**
salt
3 **eggs, separated**
7 **tablespoons whipping cream**
butter, for frying

Dissolve the yeast in 7 tablespoons of warm milk (or as per instructions on the packet) and allow the mixture to rise for 10 minutes.

Put the flour and a little salt in a large bowl and make a well in the center. Add the egg yolks to the yeast and gently whip together. Pour the mixture into the flour well. Mix well, gradually incorporating the remainder of the warm milk and cream.

Leave the batter to rest in a warm, draft-free place for an hour.

Beat the egg whites (not too stiffly) and carefully fold into the mixture with a metal spoon. The batter should be light, with bubbles on the surface.

Allow the batter to rest for a further 20 minutes.

Melt a knob of butter in a skillet and pour in a ladleful of batter, around 3/4 inch thick. Cook over low heat. When the surface of the blini is dry, flip it over with a spatula and cook the other side.

Cook the remaining blinis in the same way. Keep them warm in a preheated oven at a low temperature, wrapped in aluminum foil.

Pancakes

Makes around 12 pancakes

1³/₄ cups all-purpose flour, sifted
2 teaspoons baking powder
1 tablespoon sugar
¹/₂ teaspoon salt
1 egg, plus 2 egg whites
7 tablespoons whipping cream
2 tablespoons unsalted butter, melted
1³/₄ cups milk
butter, for frying

Mix together the flour, baking powder, sugar and salt in a bowl. In another bowl whip the whole egg vigorously with the cream, melted butter and milk. Combine the contents of the two bowls and mix thoroughly until the mixture is smooth.

Beat the egg whites (not too stiffly) and fold into the batter.

Allow the batter to stand at room temperature for an hour.

Melt a knob of butter in a small frying pan and pour in a small ladleful of batter. Cook over a moderate heat. As soon as bubbles appear on the surface, flip the pancake over with a spatula. Continue to cook until the pancake no longer sticks to the surface of the pan.

Serve hot with maple syrup or corn syrup.

English muffins

Makes 6–8 muffins

¹/₂ **envelope active dry yeast**
³/₄ **cup warm water**
1 **lb all-purpose flour, sifted**
1 **teaspoon salt**
1 **teaspoon superfine sugar**
³/₄ **cup milk**
¹/₃ **cup fine semolina flour, or durum wheat flour**

Dissolve the dried yeast in half the warm water, or as per the instructions on the packet.

Mix the flour, salt, and sugar in a bowl and make a well in the center. Pour the dissolved yeast into the well together with the milk and the remaining warm water. Work the batter until it is smooth and elastic, either by hand or using a food mixer with a paddle attachment. Continue until all the liquid has been thoroughly mixed in.

Cover with a dish towel and allow the mixture to rise in a warm place for about 1 hour.

Work the batter for a further 5 minutes and allow to rest for 30 minutes. Form into 8 balls and place them on a on a cookie sheet, sprinkled generously with fine semolina. Flatten slightly with the palm of your hand. Cover with a clean cloth and allow the dough to rise in a warm place for a further 30 minutes.

Heat an ungreased cast-iron skillet over a gentle heat and place half the muffins flat side down in the pan. Turn the muffins over during cooking. Cook for 6 minutes on each side. Keep the muffins warm while the second batch is being cooked.

Serve with butter and jam, or conserves.

Pikelets
preparation time: 15 minutes • resting time: 35 minutes • cooking time: 4 minutes per pikelet

Makes around 20 pikelets

¹/₂ envelope active dry yeast • 1 cup water • 1³/₄ cups all-purpose flour, sifted • ¹/₂ teaspoon baking powder • 1 tablespoon sugar • pinch of salt • ³/₄ cup milk • ³/₄ cup raisins

Dissolve the yeast in the warm water, or as per the instructions on the packet. Allow to rise for 10 minutes. Put the flour, baking powder, sugar, and salt in a bowl. Add the dissolved yeast and work the batter well for 2 minutes to an elastic dropping consistency.

Cover with a clean dish towel and allow to rise for 20 minutes. Gradually incorporate the milk and raisins into the batter and allow to rise for a further 15 minutes.

Heat a cast-iron or nonstick skillet. Grease with a wad of paper towels soaked in oil or smeared with butter. Pour a small amount of batter into the hot pan, which will soon form bubbles. When the top begins to set, flip the pikelet over. Cook for another minute. Repeat until the batter is used up. Serve warm with butter, honey, or maple syrup.

Crumpets
preparation time: 15 minutes • resting time: 20 minutes • cooking time: 5–10 minutes

Makes around 10 crumpets

¹/₂ envelope active dry yeast • 1¹/₄ cups water • 1³/₄ cups all-purpose flour, sifted • 1 teaspoon salt • ¹/₂ teaspoon baking powder • 7 tablespoons milk

Dissolve the yeast in the warm water, or as per the instructions on the packet. Let rise for 10 minutes. Put the flour, salt, and baking powder in a bowl and make a well in the center. Add the dissolved yeast and milk and work the mixture for 2 minutes until it has an elastic dropping consistency. Allow to rest for about 20 minutes.

Heat a cast-iron or nonstick skillet over moderate heat and put in 2 or 3 greased rings or crumpet molds, depending on the size of your pan. Pour a small amount of batter into the molds to a depth of around ¹/₄ inch. The surface should soon become covered in bubbles that will burst to create the traditional holes. (If bubbles fail to appear, thin the batter. If the batter runs under the mold, add more flour.) When the surface has set, remove the mold with a cloth and flip over. Cook for a further 3 minutes. Regrease the pan and molds, or rings, and repeat until all the batter is used up. Serve hot with butter and honey or, as a savory option, with cheese.

savory

Savory galette

Per person
**1 buckwheat galette
(see recipe page 6)**
25 g (1 oz) butter
1 thin slice cooked ham
**¼ cup grated cheese
(Emmenthal or Gruyère)**
1 fresh egg
**sea salt and freshly ground
pepper**

Prepare and cook the galette as shown on page 6.

Once it is cooked on both sides, leave in the pan and butter it generously. Lay the slice of ham in the center and sprinkle with grated cheese. Crack the egg, taking care not to break the yolk, and slide onto the ham. Season with salt and pepper.

Cook gently until the egg white is milky in color and the cheese has melted, then fold each edge of the galette towards the center, leaving the egg yolk exposed.

Add a small knob of butter and serve.

Variation
You can use cooked lean bacon instead of ham.

Walnut galette

Per person

1 buckwheat galette (see recipe page 6)

1 tablespoon unsalted butter

piece of soft goats' cheese (chèvre), around 3 inches in length

5 walnuts, roughly chopped

1 teaspoon honey

Prepare the batter as shown on page 6. When flipping the galette in the pan, place a knob of butter in the pan to ensure it is well buttered while cooking.

Cut the goats' cheese into 4 or 5 slices and place on top of the galette. Sprinkle with walnuts and cook for 2 or 3 minutes to allow the cheese to melt.

Fold the galette into a triangle, drizzle the honey over the top and allow to caramelize.

Serve immediately.

Morvan savory pancakes with bacon

Makes 6 pancakes

2²/₃ cups all-purpose flour, sifted

pinch of salt

1³/₄ cups milk

4 large eggs

10 oz bacon, rind removed and finely sliced

Put the flour and a pinch of salt in a bowl and make a well in the center. Put the milk in another bowl and beat in the eggs. Gradually add the liquid mixture to the flour and beat until the batter reaches a relatively thick but still fluid consistency.

Put 4 slices of the bacon in a skillet and once the pan is nicely greased with the melted fat, pour a ladleful of batter into the pan and cook until it sets. Flip with a spatula and cook the other side for a further 3 minutes.

Make six pancakes using this method, keeping them warm in an oven heated to 250°F.

Tips and tricks

You can use two skillets at once, if possible, to save time. This dish is a speciality from the Morvan region of Burgundy, France, where it is known as Crapiau du Morvan and was once served in place of bread. It is delicious served with soup.

Ficelles picardes

(Ham, cheese, and mushroom filled pancakes from Picardy)

Serves 5–6

For the pancake batter
1½ cups all-purpose flour, sifted
½ teaspoon salt
2 eggs
1½ cups milk
1½ cups water, or beer
3 tablespoons melted unsalted butter

For the filling
8 oz mushrooms
3 oz unsalted butter
pinch of grated nutmeg
scant ½ cup all-purpose flour, sifted
1¼ cups milk
2 tablespoons sour cream
1 cup grated Gruyère cheese
10 slices cooked ham
salt and pepper

To make the pancake batter

Put the flour and salt in a bowl and make a well in the center.

Beat the eggs in a bowl and add the milk. Pour this mixture into the well and whisk the ingredients together, combining them thoroughly. Thin the batter down with as much of the water, or beer, as necessary and add the melted butter. Allow the batter to rest for an hour.

If the batter thickens after resting, add a little milk. This quantity will make around 10 pancakes (not too thin).

To make the filling

Clean the mushrooms and slice finely. Melt 2 tablespoons of the butter in a pan over medium heat, add the mushrooms and toss until cooked. Season with salt, pepper, and a pinch of grated nutmeg.

To make the béchamel sauce, melt 2 tablespoons of butter in a small pan, add the flour and mix thoroughly. Cook on a low heat for 1 or 2 minutes and pour all the milk into the mixture in one go. Whisk vigorously and continuously until the sauce thickens and becomes smooth and velvety. Cook gently for a minute or two. Add the mushrooms and cook for a further minute. Remove from the heat and add the sour cream and grated cheese. Season with salt and pepper.

Preheat the oven to 350°F. Place a slice of ham on each pancake and cover with a layer of the mushroom sauce. Roll up the pancakes and align tightly in a greased ovenproof dish. Dot with the remaining butter and cook in the oven for 20 minutes until golden brown.

Panarea pancakes

Serves 6

**6 savory crepes
(see recipe page 18)**

6 tomatoes

1 lb ricotta cheese

**15 basil leaves, finely
chopped**

**8 oz piece mozzarella
cheese (or two balls of
mozzarella di bufala)**

2 tablespoons olive oil

**1 cup Parmesan cheese,
grated**

salt and pepper

Peel, seed, and chop the tomatoes roughly. Season with salt and
pepper.

Stir the ricotta in a bowl and add the basil.

Cut the mozzarella cheese into small dice and stir into the ricotta
and basil.

Spread the mixture over the crêpes and roll them up, but not too
tightly. Cut each rolled crêpe into 4 or 5 slices.

Preheat the oven to 350°F. Brush an ovenproof dish with a little
olive oil and lay the rolls in the dish. Cover with the tomatoes
and the remainder of the oil. Sprinkle with grated Parmesan.

Cook in the oven for 30 minutes until golden brown.

Seafood crêpes

Serves 6

**6 savory crêpes
(see recipe page 16)**

1¾ pints mussels

**1¾ pints cockles, or tiny
clams**

8 shallots

3 oz unsalted butter

12 scallops, with their coral

**3½ tablespoons all-purpose
flour**

**7 tablespoons dry white
wine**

1 cup sour cream

**a few sprigs of chives and
parsley, finely chopped**

salt and pepper

Scrape and wash the mussels.

Steep the cockles (or clams) in water and rinse well.

Peel the shallots and chop finely.

In a large pan, sweat half the shallots in 2 tablespoons of butter. Add all the shellfish and the parsley then cover. Shake the pan from time to time to ensure even cooking. When the shells have opened, remove them and strain the cooking juice through a fine strainer and reserve. Set aside the mussels and cockles, or clams, discarding any that have not opened.

Melt 2 tablespoons of butter in a pan and cook the rest of the shallots gently until golden.

Cut the scallops into 3 or 4 pieces and add to the pan. Sauté rapidly over a high heat for 1 minute on each side. Season and set aside.

Melt the rest of the butter, add the flour and cook for several minutes without browning until the mixture foams. Add the strained shellfish juice, the wine, and the sour cream. Beat well until the sauce becomes smooth. Adjust the seasoning, add the chives and quickly reheat the shellfish in the sauce.

Reheat the crepes, either in a pan with a little butter or by steaming them on a plate over a pan of boiling water, then fill with the seafood sauce.

Serve immediately.

Chestnut blinis with salmon caviar

Serves 4

¹/₂ **envelope active dry yeast**

³/₄ **cup milk**

1³/₄ **cups chestnut flour** (*farine de chataignes*)

4 **eggs, separated**

³/₄ **cup whipping cream**

pinch of salt

butter, for frying

To serve

sour cream

salmon caviar

Allow the yeast to rise in a little tepid milk, or as per instructions on the packet, then add the rest of the milk. Gradually beat in the chestnut flour, alternating each addition with an egg yolk. When all the flour and eggs are amalgamated, add the cream and a pinch of salt.

Cover the batter with a cloth and leave to stand in a warm place for two hours.

Beat the 4 egg whites into fairly soft peaks so that they will incorporate smoothly into the rather liquid batter. Fold them into the mixture, which should be light, with little bubbles rising to the surface.

Melt a little knob of butter in a small skillet and pour in a layer of batter around 1 inch thick. Cook over a low heat. When the underside of the blini is set turn it with a spatula and cook the other side.

Cook the rest of the blinis in the same way, until all the batter has been used, keeping them warm in an preheated oven at the lowest temperature, covered in aluminum foil.

Serve with sour cream and salmon caviar.

Potato and mushroom blinis

Serves 6

1¼ lb floury potatoes

½ envelope active dry yeast

1 cup all-purpose flour, sifted

1 lb wild mushrooms (cèpes, chanterelles, etc)

1 tablespoon oil

To serve

1 stalk flatleaf parsley, finely chopped

few sprigs of chervil, finely chopped

melted butter

To make the batter

Cut the potatoes into large pieces and cook in boiling salted water until they no longer resist the point of a knife. Drain well, shaking the colander several times. Leave to cool.

Dissolve the yeast in 1¼ cups water, or as per instructions on the packet, until risen.

Peel the potatoes and mash well in a bowl. Add the flour and the yeast and mix well. Add sufficient warm water to make a rather thick batter.

Cover with a cloth and leave to stand for 1 hour.

To prepare the mushrooms

Trim the stalks of the mushrooms and clean them with a little brush, being careful not to let them come directly under running water. Dry them with a damp cloth if necessary and slice thinly.

Heat the oil in a large pan over high heat and add the mushrooms. Turn the heat down and simmer until all their water has evaporated, then drain.

Cook the blinis in one or more small pans to save time, and keep warm.

Put a spoonful of mushrooms on each blini, sprinkle with parsley and chervil, and serve with melted butter on the side.

Buckwheat blinis with smoked haddock

Serves 6

2 cups milk

$1/2$ envelope active dry yeast

scant cup buckwheat flour

$1^1/3$ cups all-purpose flour, sifted

$1/2$ teaspoon salt

$3^1/2$ tablespoons whipping cream

3 eggs, separated

To serve

6 thick slices smoked haddock

$3/4$ cup sour cream, lightly whipped

few sprigs of dill, chopped

Warm half the milk and dissolve the yeast in it, or as per instructions on the packet. Leave to rise.

Mix both the flours and the salt together in a bowl and make a well in the center.

Add the whipping cream to the remainder of the milk, heat gently and add to the yeast. Beat a spoonful of this mixture into the flour, followed by an egg yolk, repeating until the egg yolks are used up. Add the rest of the liquid and beat until the batter is smooth and runny.

Cover the bowl and leave to stand in a warm place for 2 hours.

Whisk the egg whites into stiff peaks and fold into the batter.

Cook the blinis following the instructions given in the recipe on page 8.

Serve topped with a slice of smoked haddock and the lightly whipped sour cream. Sprinkle with chopped dill.

Zucchini pancakes

Makes around 12 pancakes
1 cup pumpkin flesh
2 zucchini
3 eggs
few chives, finely chopped
few chervil leaves
pinch of grated nutmeg
scant ½ cup all-purpose flour, sifted
1 teaspoon baking powder
2 tablespoons oil
1 oz unsalted butter
salt and pepper

To serve
poached eggs
pumpkin seeds

Grate the pumpkin. Trim the ends of the zucchini but leave the skin on. Grate them very finely.

Using your hands, squeeze out the juice and put the flesh in a bowl. Add the eggs, herbs, salt and pepper, nutmeg, and finally the flour and baking powder. Mix well.

Leave to stand in a cold place for 30 minutes.

Melt the oil and butter together in a skillet over low heat. Use several little pans if possible, as the pancakes take some time to cook (around 3 minutes each side), or use a large pan that will hold 3 or 4 pancakes at once. When the fat is hot add a ladleful of batter and cook until the underside is golden-brown and you can lift the pancakes with a spatula. Turn over and cook for 5–7 minutes more.

Serve with poached eggs or scatter pumpkin seeds and a few chervil leaves instead of vegetables.

Corn pancakes

Makes around 12 pancakes

1 cup canned corn
2 cups milk
1½ cups all-purpose flour, sifted
1 teaspoon baking powder
1 teaspoon salt
2 tablespoons lemon juice
1 egg
4 tablespoons melted unsalted butter
butter, for frying

To serve
scrambled eggs
melted butter

Purée the corn with a little milk.

Mix the flour, baking powder, and salt together in a bowl and make a well in the center.

In another bowl, stir the rest of the milk and the lemon juice together, then add the egg, corn purée and the melted butter.

Pour this mixture into the flour and beat until it forms a smooth batter.

Leave to stand for 1 hour at room temperature.

Melt a little knob of butter in a small pan and pour in a ladleful of batter. Cook the pancake over a gentle heat until the underside begins to turn brown, then turn it with a spatula. Continue cooking until the batter no longer sticks to the pan, which indicates that it is ready.

Serve simply with scrambled eggs or melted butter.

sweet

Crêpes dentelles

Makes around 20 crêpes

1³/₄ cups all-purpose flour, sifted

1 generous cup superfine sugar

good pinch of salt

4 eggs

3 cups milk

4 tablespoons melted unsalted butter

vanilla extract (optional)

butter, for frying

Mix together the flour, sugar, and salt in a bowl and make a well in the center.

Beat the eggs and add the milk, melted butter, and vanilla extract, if using.

Pour the mixture into the bowl of flour and beat well to obtain a smooth batter.

Melt a little knob of butter in a well-heated crêpe pan and pour in a small quantity of batter. Coat the entire surface evenly (see Tips and Tricks, page 4) and, as soon as the crêpe begins to change color, roll it up. Do this quickly to avoid burning your fingers!

If you want to eat the crêpe whole allow it to cool a bit, otherwise cut it into several pieces while still hot.

Store in an airtight container in a cool dry place.

Apple crêpes caramelized with butter

Per person
1 crêpe (see recipe page 7)
1 small apple
1 oz butter
2 tablespoons sugar

Peel, core, and slice the apple.

Melt 1 tablespoon of butter in a pan over a high heat and add the apple slices. Dredge with sugar and cook until the fruit is thoroughly caramelized. Remove the apple slices and set aside in a warm place. Deglaze the pan with a half-glass of water, scraping well. Set the caramel glaze aside.

Make the crêpe following the basic recipe and spread with the remaining butter. Reheat the glaze. Top the pancake with a spoonful of caramelized apples and pour over the glaze.

Fold and serve immediately

Variation
Sprinkle the apples with cinnamon and deglaze the pan with Calvados.

Crêpes Suzette

Serves 6–8 (makes around 18 crêpes)

For the batter

1¾ cups all-purpose flour, sifted

½ cup sugar

2 oz unsalted butter

3 eggs

good pinch salt

1¾ cups milk

¾ cup water, or beer

a little orange-flower water

For the filling

5 oz unsalted butter, at room temperature

zest of 1 orange, finely grated

¾ cup superfine sugar

To serve

7 tablespoons orange liqueur (Grand-Marnier, Cointreau, Curaçao)

1 tablespoon confectioners' sugar

To make the batter

Put the flour and sugar in a bowl and make a well in the center. Melt the butter in a small pan. In another bowl, beat the eggs lightly with the salt. Gradually add the eggs and milk to the flour, and mix with a wire whisk to blend well. Add the water, or beer, and the melted butter. Refrigerate for at least 2 hours. If the batter has thickened after standing, dilute it with a little milk. The batter can be flavored with a few drops of orange-flower water.

Make around 18–20 very thin crepes in a lightly buttered medium-sized pan. Stack them as you go along to keep them soft.

To make the filling

Cream the softened butter with the orange zest, add the superfine sugar and 1 tablespoon of the orange liqueur.

Spread a thin layer of this cream over each crêpe, fold it into a triangle and arrange the crêpes in a fan shape in an ovenproof dish. Reheat in the oven at 210°F for 10 minutes before serving. Warm the remaining liqueur in a small pan over low heat.

Bring the crêpes to the table, dredge them with confectioners' sugar, and pour over the warmed liqueur. Set alight and spoon the flaming liqueur over the crêpes until the flames die down. Serve immediately.

Variation

Replace the orange with a mandarin and the liqueur with Mandarin liqueur.

Russian crêpes stuffed with fromage blanc

Serves 6

For the batter
1⅓ **cups all-purpose flour, sifted**
4 **tablespoons sugar**
1½ **oz unsalted butter**
2 **eggs**
a good pinch of salt
¾ **cup milk**
¾ **cup water, or beer**
1 **teaspoon vanilla extract**

For the filling
2 **egg yolks**
½ **cup sugar**
1 **cup fromage blanc, or ricotta cheese (well drained)**
1 **vanilla bean**
⅓ **cup diced candied fruit**
½ **cup slivered almonds**
3 **tablespoons sour cream**

Make a dozen crêpes following the recipe on page 36, but using vanilla extract in place of orange-flower water.

To make the filling

Beat together the egg yolks and ⅓ cup of the sugar until the mixture turns pale. Add the cheese. Split open the vanilla bean lengthways and scrape the seeds into the batter with the tip of a knife.

Mix in gently and add the candied fruit and the slivered almonds.

Preheat the oven to 350°F.

Fill the crêpes with the mixture and fold each into a fan shape.

Put the crêpes in a buttered dish and spread over the sour cream. Sprinkle with the rest of the sugar and put in the preheated oven. Leave to caramelize for 20–30 minutes.

Serve warm or cold.

Gâteau of crêpes with lemon

Serves 6–8

For the batter
1¹⁄₃ cups all-purpose flour, sifted
4 tablespoons sugar
1¹⁄₂ oz unsalted butter
2 eggs
a good pinch of salt
1 ¹⁄₄ cups milk
7 tablespoons water, or beer
zest of one lemon, finely grated

For the lemon cream
3 lemons
3 eggs
⁷⁄₈ cup sugar
3 oz butter

To serve
confectioners' sugar
a few redcurrants
a *coulis* of red berries

Prepare the batter following the recipe on page 36, but using the lemon zest in place of the orange-flower water. Make around 15 thin crêpes.

To make the lemon cream

Peel the zest from 1 lemon, avoiding as much pith as possible and cut into strips. Squeeze the juice from all 3 lemons.

Break the eggs into a pan, add the sugar, lemon juice, and zest and heat gently, stirring constantly. The mixture will thicken and gradually turn creamy. Remove from the heat just before it reaches boiling point and pass through a strainer to remove the zest. While the mixture is still warm, add the butter cut into small pieces and blend in.

Preheat the oven to 340°F.

Butter a mold or ring of the same diameter as the crêpes. Put the first crêpe in the mold and spread with a thin layer of lemon cream. Top with another crêpe and repeat until all the ingredients have been used, finishing with a crêpe.

Place in the oven and cook for around 20 minutes. Leave to cool before turning out.

Sprinkle with confectioners' sugar. Garnish with redcurrants or serve with a *coulis* of red berries.

Crêpes with pear soufflé filling

Serves 6

For the batter

1⅓ cups all-purpose flour, sifted

4 tablespoons sugar

1½ oz unsalted butter

2 eggs

pinch of salt

¾ cup milk

¾ cup water, or beer

For the filling

3 tablespoons cornstarch

¾ cup milk

4 tablespoons superfine sugar

4 eggs, separated

1 oz unsalted butter

2 ripe pears, peeled and diced finely

a little pear eau-de-vie

3 tablespoons confectioners' sugar

To serve

confectioners' sugar

a *coulis* of red berries

Make six crêpes, each around 8 inches in diameter, following the instructions given on page 36, but omitting the orange-flower water.

To make the filling

Blend the cornstarch with 3 tablespoons cold milk. Bring the rest of the milk to the boil with 1½ tablespoons of sugar.

Stir the blended cornstarch into the hot milk and return to the heat. Beat the mixture constantly until it thickens, without letting it reach boiling point.

Remove from the heat and stir in the 4 egg yolks and the butter. Transfer to a large bowl and put in the refrigerator to chill.

Whisk the egg whites until they form firm peaks, adding the remaining sugar halfway through. Fold gently into the cold milk and egg mixture. Add the diced pears and the pear eau-de-vie.

Preheat the oven to 400°F.

Fill each crêpe with a portion of the mixture and fold in two like a half moon.

Arrange the crêpes in an ovenproof dish, dust with confectioners' sugar and bake in the oven for 5 minutes, or until the soufflé mixture rises.

Remove from the oven and serve immediately with a dusting of icing sugar. Try serving with a red berry *coulis*.

'Beggar's purses' with chocolate

Serves 6

For the crêpe batter

1⅓ cups all-purpose flour, sifted

4 tablespoons sugar

1½ oz unsalted butter

2 eggs

good pinch of salt

¾ cup milk

¾ cup water, or beer

For the filling

7 oz best-quality dark chocolate, continental if possible

2 eggs, separated

¾ cup whipping cream

1 orange

2 tablespoons sugar

To serve

½ cup slivered almonds, toasted

light stirred custard sauce, or cream of your choice

Make 6 large crêpes, following the instructions on page 36, but omitting the orange-flower water. Keep warm in a plate over a pan of boiling water.

To make the chocolate mousse

Break the chocolate into small pieces and melt in a microwave or in a bowl over a pan of barely simmering water. Remove from the heat, cool slightly and add the egg yolks, one at a time.

Whip the cream lightly and whisk the egg whites until stiff. Stir the cream into the chocolate–egg mixture, then gently fold in the egg whites with a metal spoon. Refrigerate for at least 6 hours.

Scrub and dry the orange. Peel off the zest in strips about ⅛ inch wide. Place in a small pan with the sugar and a little water over a low heat and leave to candy for 10 minutes.

To assemble the 'beggar's purses'

Put a dollop of chocolate mousse in the center of each crêpe and tie up the 'purse' with a strip of orange zest, being careful not to break it. Repeat with the remaining crêpes.

Scatter with slivered almonds and serve with a light stirred custard sauce, or cream.

Tip

This dessert is best assembled at the last minute.

Apple turnover

Serves 6

For the batter

3 eggs

1½ **cups all-purpose flour, sifted**

2 **tablespoons melted unsalted butter**

2 **cups milk**

4 **tablespoons sugar**

pinch of salt

For the filling

3 **eating apples**

generous ⅓ **cup sugar**

2 **oz unsalted butter**

small glass of Calvados

To make the batter

Whisk the eggs to a froth, mix in the flour, melted butter, milk, sugar, and salt.

Leave to rest for 30 minutes.

To prepare the filling

Peel and core the apples and slice thinly. Sprinkle with 4 tablespoons of the sugar, shaking to make sure they are well covered.

Melt half the butter in a large skillet (nonstick if possible) and pour in 2 ladlefuls of batter. As soon as it begins to set spread over the apple slices and, after a few seconds, pour in the rest of the batter. Cook over a low heat, shaking the pan regularly so that the bottom doesn't stick. Turn the crêpe over onto a plate and add the remaining butter to the pan, then slide the crêpe back into the pan and continue cooking until this side is nicely golden.

Put the crêpe on a heat-resistant serving dish.

Sprinkle the crêpe with the remaining sugar and flame it with the prewarmed Calvados.

Cut into slices and serve immediately.

Jam parcels

Serves 6
(makes around
12 parcels)

For the batter

1⅓ cups all-purpose flour, sifted

½ cup sugar

1½ oz unsalted butter

2 eggs

good pinch of salt

1¾ cups milk

1 drop almond essence

1 teaspoon vanilla extract

For the filling

1 jar jam, about 14 oz, as preferred (it should be fairly chunky, so avoid jellies)

2 tablespoons superfine sugar

To serve

3 tablespoons confectioners' sugar, for dusting

fruit salad

Make 12 dessert crêpes, following the recipe on page 36 but omitting the water and orange-flower water. Allow to cool.

Place a spoonful of jam in the center of each one and fold into a square envelope shape.

Arrange the crêpe parcels side by side in an ovenproof dish with the folded sides underneath and sprinkle with superfine sugar. Put under a preheated grill until the crêpes begin to glaze over.

Dust with confectioners' sugar and serve immediately with a portion of fruit salad.

Caprinettes

Makes 6 caprinettes

**8 oz fresh goats' cheese
(chèvre)**

2 eggs

**2 tablespoons melted
butter**

**1⅓ cups all-purpose flour,
sifted**

**⅔ cup fine semolina,
or durum wheat flour**

2½ cups dry white wine

pinch of salt

butter, for frying

To serve

honey

Mash the cheese with a fork.

Stir in the eggs and the melted butter, and thin with half the white wine.

Mix the flour, semolina, and salt in a bowl then gradually beat in the cheese–wine mixture. Stretch the batter with the remaining white wine and a little water, if necessary. It should be fairly liquid.

Leave to rest for at least 1 hour.

Heat a pan and grease it with a little knob of butter. Pour in a small amount of the batter and proceed as for ordinary crêpes.

Serve by themselves or drizzled with honey.

Swedish crêpes with lingonberry compote

Serves 6

For the batter

1½ cups all-purpose flour, sifted

2 tablespoons sugar

pinch of salt

2 eggs

2 cups milk

1 teaspoon vanilla extract

For the filling

14 oz lingonberries: fresh, vacuum-packed or frozen (or use cranberries as an alternative)

½ cup sugar

butter for frying

To serve

confectioners' sugar

First make the lingonberry compote by cooking the berries with the sugar over a low heat for 10–15 minutes until all the juice has evaporated.

Put the flour, sugar, and salt in a bowl. Make a well in the center, break in the eggs and pour in the milk and vanilla extract. Gradually incorporate the flour, continuously bringing it towards the center until it makes a smooth and runny batter.

Heat a little butter in a pan and ladle in a small quantity of batter. Cook for 1–2 minutes then turn the crêpe. Each side should be cooked fairly quickly so that the crêpes remain creamy.

Stack the crêpes on a plate as you go along, cover with aluminum foil and keep warm in an oven preheated to the lowest temperature.

When ready to serve, fill the crêpes with compote and dust with confectioners' sugar.

Note

Lingonberries are relatives of cranberries and are grown in many Scandinavian countries. If they are not available, use cranberries as an alternative.

Bouquettes liégeoises with raisins

**Makes around
10** *bouquettes*
½ **envelope active dry yeast**
¾ **cup buckwheat flour**
**1 cup all-purpose flour,
sifted**
½ **teaspoon cinnamon**
1 egg
½ **cup raisins**
a good pinch of salt
butter, for frying

To serve
light molasses

Dissolve the yeast in tepid water, or as per the instructions on the packet, and allow to rise.

Mix both the flours together with the cinnamon and the salt in a bowl. Add the egg and the yeast and mix thoroughly until all lumps have gone. Thin the batter with some warm water to obtain a smooth, fluid consistency, then add the raisins.

Cover the batter and leave to rise in a draught-proof place until the raisins come to the surface.

Melt a knob of butter in a medium pan and cook the *bouquettes*, flipping them over once.

Serve with light molasses for dipping.

Goanese banana pancakes

Serves 4

1 cup all-purpose flour, sifted

1 teaspoon baking powder

1 tablespoon vanilla sugar, (or superfine sugar with a drop of vanilla extract)

1 egg

7 tablespoons milk

2/3 cup coconut milk

2 tablespoons rum

2 small bananas

1/3 cup soft dark brown sugar

grated coconut

butter, for frying

Mix the flour, baking powder, and vanilla sugar in a bowl.

In another bowl, whisk together the egg, milk, and coconut milk. Stir in the rum.

Pour the liquid into the flour mixture and beat vigorously to obtain a smooth batter. Leave to rest for 30 minutes at room temperature.

Peel the bananas and slice into rounds.

Melt a small knob of butter in a medium pan and pour in a quarter of the batter. Cook the pancake over a gentle heat and, as soon as the underside begins to brown, turn it with a spatula. Cover with a layer of sliced banana and sprinkle with dark brown sugar and grated coconut. Continue cooking until the batter is cooked and no longer sticks to the pan.

Fold the pancake over and serve immediately.

Tip

Use ripe, fragrant bananas for this dish.

Apple pancakes

Makes 6–8 pancakes

3 eggs
³/₄ cup milk
1¹/₄ cups all-purpose flour, sifted
1 tablespoon sugar
¹/₂ teaspoon cinnamon
¹/₂ teaspoon baking powder
pinch of salt
2 eating apples
butter, for frying

To serve
confectioners' sugar or smoked bacon

Beat the eggs lightly and add the milk.

Mix together the flour, sugar, cinnamon, baking powder, and salt in a bowl. Pour in the egg–milk mixture and beat well to obtain a smooth batter.

Allow to stand in the refrigerator.

Peel the apples and slice into thin slices.

Melt a small knob of butter in a pan and cook a few apple slices until golden-brown. As soon as they are done, pour a little batter over and cook until it begins to set and spot. Turn with a spatula and cook for a further 1–2 minutes. Repeat until all the apples and batter are used up.

Serve hot, dredged with confectioners' sugar or, more daringly, with a slice of smoked bacon.

Yogurt and blueberry pancakes

Makes 6–8 pancakes
1½ cups all-purpose flour, sifted
1 tablespoon superfine sugar
1 teaspoon baking powder
pinch of salt
1 egg
4 tablespoons melted butter
²/₃ cup plain yogurt
7 tablespoons water
¾ cup fresh blueberries
butter, for frying

To serve
whipped cream

In a bowl, mix together the flour, sugar, baking powder, and salt.

In another bowl, beat together the egg, melted butter, and yogurt. When thoroughly mixed, thin with a little water.

Pour the liquid mix into the dry ingredients and beat to obtain a smooth batter.

Stir in the blueberries, being careful not to crush them.

Leave to rest for 1 hour.

Melt a little knob of butter in a small pan and pour in a small ladleful of batter. Cook the pancake over medium heat, and as soon as the underside begins to turn brown, flip it over with a spatula. Cook until the batter has set, which shows the pancake is ready.

Serve hot with whipped cream.

Spicy pancakes

Makes 6–8 pancakes

1¾ cups whole-wheat flour

¾ cup soft light brown sugar

1 cup pecan nuts, finely chopped, reserving a few for decoration

1 teaspoon baking powder

grated nutmeg

powdered cinnamon

½ teaspoon salt

2 eggs

2 tablespoons melted butter

2½ cups milk

butter, for frying

To serve

maple syrup

Put the flour, sugar, chopped pecans, baking powder, spices, and salt in a bowl and mix well.

In another bowl, lightly beat the eggs and the melted butter. Gradually add the milk.

Blend both mixtures together carefully and leave to stand for 1 hour.

Cook as for the classic pancake, following the basic recipe on page 9.

Serve warm, with maple syrup.

Chocolate blinis with *marrons glacés* ice-cream

Serves 6

1 envelope active dry yeast

2 cups milk

1¾ cups sifted all-purpose flour

¾ cup buckwheat flour

7 tablespoons cocoa

pinch of salt

2 teaspoons superfine sugar

⅔ cup whipping cream

3 eggs, separated

4 tablespoons melted butter

butter, for frying

For the chocolate sauce

300 ml (½ pint) milk

3½ oz best-quality dark chocolate, continental if possible

For the *marrons glacés* ice cream

around 9 oz canned sweetened chestnut purée

2 tablespoons single cream

1 cup whipping cream

6 tablespoons confectioners' sugar

Dissolve the yeast in a glass of tepid milk, or as per the instructions on the packet, and allow to rise.

Mix together both the flours, the cocoa, salt, and sugar.

Mix the rest of the milk and the cream together and warm slightly. Add to the diluted yeast. Gradually incorporate this mixture into the dry ingredients, alternating with an egg yolk, until the ingredients have been used up. The batter should be smooth and fluid. Cover and leave to rise in a warm place for an hour.

Whisk the egg whites into fairly soft peaks and fold carefully into the batter. Lastly, stir in the melted butter and leave to rest for another 30 minutes.

To make the sauce, heat the milk, break in the chocolate and stir with a spatula until it melts smoothly. Keep warm.

Cook the blinis following the instructions given in the basic recipe on page 8. Keep them warm in a preheated oven, wrapped in aluminum foil, until the last moment.

To serve, put one or two scoops of *marrons glacés* ice-cream on each plate, add a blini and drizzle with the chocolate sauce.

To make the *marrons glacés* ice cream

Mix the purée and the single cream together in a bowl until smooth. In a separate bowl beat the whipping cream until thick but not stiff, and add the sugar. Add to the purée mixture and thoroughly mix together. Transfer to an ice-cream maker and follow the manufacturer's instructions, or pour into a freezer container and leave to set in the freezer uncovered for around 3 hours, making sure you frequently turn the sides of the mixture to the center in order to keep it creamy. Once firm, cover and transfer to the refrigerator 30 minutes before serving.